P9-CSA-891

ANOTHER NAME FOR BRIDGE

ANOTHER NAME FOR BRIDGE

Suzanne Hancock

Mansfield Press

Copyright © Suzanne Hancock 2005
All Rights Reserved
Printed in Canada

Library and Archives Canada Cataloguing in Publication

Hancock, Suzanne, 1971–
        Another name for bridge / Suzanne Hancock.

Poems.
ISBN 1-894469-22-4

        I. Title.

PS8565.A572A65 2005   C811'.54   C2005-901927-1

Design: Denis De Klerck, Rick O'Brien, Marijke Friesen
Cover Photo: Stefan Schmuhl

The publication of Another Name for Bridge
has been generously supported by
The Canada Council for the Arts and
The Ontario Arts Council.

Mansfield Press Inc.
25 Mansfield Avenue, Toronto, Ontario, Canada M6J 2A9
Publisher: Denis De Klerck
www.mansfieldpress.net

For Barzin
For Ray & Joyce Hancock
and
in memory of
Michael Harrington
1932 – 2005

CONTENTS

One

Two

ONE

Listen. If I have known beauty
let's say I came to it
asking

Oh?

Phyllis Webb

SELF DECEIT

That love is swollen and vascular.
That it is a bridge holding two torsos immobile.
A way to afford the heat.

Wind lifts the wrapping paper,
pulls and pulls until it flutters wildly,
the box underneath smooth and
bone-china white.

That the body is as civil as cedar
and if you build a fire of welcome
someone will see. Will come.

Just hold out your merciful hands
and they will be filled.
History in its steaming cup,
all the proof you need.

A DRUNK'S DAUGHTER

Not only at night at The Spun Arrow. Always lunch meetings and the front seat of his polished truck, always when the lights went out and birthday candles were lit, or the bride, after a chorus of silver on crystal, leaned over to kiss the groom. Once, in high school she stood in front of a dozen boys and drank vodka from plastic glasses. The clear liquid the boys winced and gagged on she drank without a grimace, with only a slight warming of her belly. *My father fills himself up with this* she said to no one. Years later, after his insides almost gave out and he had to stop, they had dinner near the ocean. While they sat she watched his body get up and walk out the front door. She watched him straddle a barstool and lift a short ice-filled glass to his grateful lips. She knew that he was not there in front of her, that he had not been for a long time, and as he wiped his ruined mouth with the white napkin, she almost forgave him for everything.

CONVERSION

That's a gorgeous piece of beef
the guests always said with feeling. A roast,
bougainvillea-pink in the center, and a

drizzle of gravy hidden under a napkin,
after a Sunday park-walk. She always loved
the underdog, the smallest boy on the field

in cleats, a continual swath of green
between him and the ball as the bigger boys kicked
it this way and that, the squirrel with a twisted

leg, hungry. If she piled potatoes
on the slice of meat her mother centered on
the plate she could imagine a natural death,

the animal quietly closing its eyes
in a blizzard, blood slowing on its way back
to the heart from the spotted flanks: I will lie

down now. I will die. Under the long
tablecloth a guest's son would rub his calf
against hers as he sawed through the flesh

then lifted it to his waiting mouth.
At the end of the night, before the food on
the counter was wrapped in plastic and stacked

in the fridge, they'd all stand near
the closet fitting coats onto bodies and she'd
hold her breath when they'd come to her

with tainted kisses, the gorgeous
cow between their teeth. She'd wash her
mouth out. Then ask for forgiveness.

THE POEM AS YARD SALE

You're certainly not doing it
for the money: that becomes
clear when you imagine the weight
of two quarters in your palm
as you hand over the memory of
the slow-speaking man from Madrid
who gave you the miniature bronze
candelabra that has been in the bottom
desk drawer for years. Or a dime
for the grateful noise that child uttered
at a table in front of the grocery store
when you said yes to the tiny glass vase
that would send him to summer camp.
People will pull up in their cars
and finger your too-small winter
coats, the stale scent of the boxed
collection of Agatha Christie paperbacks
you stole from someone's trash
last summer, the red skirt ripped
a little along the back seam.
Your unwanted, unused
life splayed in front of you.
And as you arrange the trinkets
and memories into attractive groupings
down the concrete stairs, across
the gently-sloped green of the lawn,
how much can you get rid of
before the moments contained within
everything get up and walk away,
held tightly in someone else's hand?

THE TREE

My mother drove off in her two-tone red Chevrolet and I climbed the tree. What are two small feet supposed to do on the ground without a mother? On the clothesline my nightgown. My eye on the corner where she would turn from the big street-artery onto our minor avenue but it was never her. Sometimes Mr. Ogawa in his quick clean convertible. Sometimes Mrs. Davis pushing red-haired Sean in the buggy. Salmon return home by scent. I thought the perfume of my nightgown might lead her back. In the rain it looked hunched and bony. At night my father hauled me down from the branches with a clinking metal ladder. It was hard for him, as he'd stopped eating. He'd carry the ladder with both hands and have to rest on the lawn halfway from the gate. Eventually he just left it leaning against the trunk. Neighborhood kids walked by with their schoolbooks and lunch-kits and asked what I was doing. I'd say *just waiting*. When the leaves fell in a bloody pool at my feet the jays from the top branch flew south. They turned down the wide street and that was it. I cut down the nest. Brought it inside and slept.

FIRST DAY OF HUNTING SEASON

It's only now, upon seeing them, you know they're missing:

> this morning's collection draped over concrete
>> before the frosted-glass doors of the gun store,
> dozens of graceless remains, near foolish,
>> lined up on Main Street,
>>> collapsed like that into their deaths.

> Seasonal sun warms the mute flanks.
>> A whole herd of men gleam and gloat,
>>> shoot full rolls of colour film.

And you think:
>> the medicine of those humming deer,
>>> holes burnt right through.

> And you think:
>>> as if the boundless, greenbrown world has
>> fallen in on itself.

That whole day the sun is an unsettling orange wound.

ON LION'S GATE BRIDGE

on a rented bike with a cranky bell
that sounds more like goose-pain
than luminous, ringing metal—

it's November, my knuckles are chilled
and the gnarled streak of mountains
in front of me hushes, no longer spring's

restless green, simply rail-tie gray
and a little sad in this light.
This is the bridge my mother crossed

when she moved north
and the one on which my brother's car died
in rush hour. He sat reading the paper

as he waited for help, each furious car
behind him resounding with advice
on how he could go fuck himself.

A boat like a leaf glides elegantly
below, perhaps the captain is thinking how frail
the slated bridge looks suspended above,

perhaps he's draining black coffee
from a thermos and calculating in his head
how many more Chinook and Coho it will take

to pay the mortgage this year.
It's only up here, hanging like this,
that I'm fixed to what I've left. This light and dark,

this wind that slips always through the city.
There's not much more to do here than follow
the salt current with my eye. And imagine the route

back through the park and along Burrard
to the room in my brother's apartment where
my suitcase sits open on a chair against the wall.

WAKING EARLY IN A NEW HOUSE

is like finding your way around a body
you've not touched before. There are buckles
you don't know the mechanics of, buttons

that slip away from their buttonholes
more easily than you're used to. The
air is different, and the windows lock

with a round latch at the top, not a wooden
stick placed along the bug-filled sill.
So, slowly and blindly you move

your fingers along the soft crook of the
underarm, across the chest to the neck,
then lips, like dragging your palm along

the wall looking for a doorframe. Maybe you
will eventually remember that the left hip
creaks a little under too much weight. And

the throaty vibration coming from the
kitchen is just the fridge humming in one
of Beethoven's minor keys.

Light through trees dapples differently
on these floorboards. The birds sound amplified,
more confident, though in the pliant grass

they look the same as the sparrows from the
old neighborhood. Perhaps it's the fresh paint,
or the morning, perhaps it's you.

THE DOGS

There are so many. Stretched in shapes
across the kitchen floor, out on the porch
against the white painted railing.

She is in the ripe room upstairs
too sick to swing her legs
onto the carpet below, so her husband
feeds the animals and fills their bowls
with water, wipes the charcoal sleep from their eyes.

Mornings, after flying from the porch stairs
into the moist grass the dogs surround her bed,
lick at their legs, sniff the edge of the wool blanket
covering her slight body, the only thing that keeps her
from floating up and away.

Even with the windows open the afternoon
heats the room like a weighty slap
and the dogs slip downstairs again
one after the other, tongues long, eyes flagging
under some terrible weight. They sag against
the linoleum, whine to be let outside.

The dogs were waiting for something, for an evening
when she'd pull on her boots and they'd pull
in excitement at her strong hand on the leash or
try desperately to catch up. They rub against his legs
under the kitchen table as he writes letters to those
she spoke of, to those who should be told.

THE POEM AS OPEN DOOR FACING SOUTH

HEALTH

For Brian

After he drove off with the carcass
squeezed into the back of his truck—
four dustbowl-colored legs that didn't quite fit
knocking against the starboard lip of the Ford—
the road was quiet.

Like your car and the cottontail rabbit,
its body still lithe and ticking as you scooped it into your hands,
blood and all,
placed it in the trunk thinking your brother
the vet would know what to do.

The man filets the flanks with a broad
hunting knife, thanks someone for
his luck,
the prayer something like: *Washtenaw Roads, Michigan Fall.*

Your brother says internal bleeding
so you wrap the creature in a
soft towel from the guest bathroom
attach a hose to the tailpipe, fit both into the trunk.

The moon looks on both roads
silent and overexposed.

WAYS TO MOURN

I.

Arched like a bamboo bridge bellied over water. Feel the pull,
the way water bubbles quickly underneath
        while you are motionless.

        Wooden.

2.

With the lightness of a cricket;
                bounding

                      weightless.

As if the grass were supposed to be this dry. This scorched.

3.

Elephant-like.

        Head swinging back and forth.

Heavy-foot the ground over and over. Weep loudly then

        bury it.

4.

Make new friends.　　　Change your name.　　　Rarely (if ever)
ring the wet bell of grief. Fix the smile. Don't read Rilke or Plath.
Stare empty-eyed when accidentally meeting an old neighbour at
the movie theatre.　　　*Yes, everything is perfect.*
Ignore the look she offers the back of your head.

APIARY

So close to the white screened box, a winged
thorn lands on my eyelid. The whole class watches

    my hands to see if they flutter
        upward or remain stiff
            at my sides as the woman
                in white gloves warned.

Tiny legs branched and inquisitive, like
        a trickle of water. Not a whiff
    of honey to be had.

        All those things that
        can't be seen,
      those moments so close to the earth—

warnings, null and void.

      My arms pointed down,
I wait for the sting.

OAK APPLE

The wasps are quiet at night,
their tree swollen and alone.

Once, years ago,
a plum-size growth in the flesh

beneath your breast,
now, a grapefruit in the smooth ground

of your thigh.

As if your body were a vine or a fruit-branch.

In the oak tree, wasps work diligently on the
architecture of the lump.

Each night, you say:
my cells have been busy.

RAPTURE

for TL

The more rabid the joy, the quicker
the ascent.

Think geese fleeing winter. Legs tucked tight
against speckled

bodies, the wing-flap, then slow lift into an
arrow of

feathered coins scattered against
sky.

Judgment may slur by and bodies may
rise

weightless as Catherine of Siena's after
weeks in

the dark, famished, waiting out God's phosphorescence.
Winters are long

here. On a street corner a woman watches
a cedar fence drink hours

of rain. It gleams. The wood swells. It may, indeed, pour
on the day

of rapture. The world would then be soft
and the ones

left standing on lawns, pavement, would have
something cool to drink

while those who rise glance down and wonder if they are leaving
anything behind.

SELF DECEIT

I was the only one born that day.
They all said I was the softest baby
                    in the ward, the sky above,
                              a coarse spring blue.

We went home and
everyone slept.   They called me
                    ladybug and *goldfish*

and we all slept
some more.   Some kissed me and
                              then said "it's time"

    and they told me about roads
and the robins that ticked along the grass
              each dewy morning.

One day I thought I too would be a cave
                    warm enough
                              to grow another.

Two

Sursum corda.
Habemus ad Dominum!

APPLE TREES

A wounded man, but charming.

I'd hold the basket while he tossed
the meaty red planets from the
twisted branches, his voice displaced

and lost in leaf. Most were keepers
but if a rotten one tumbled from the sky
I'd remove it quickly, before it had

a chance to spoil the bunch. Once,
an army of yellowish worms,
and me on my knees throwing

each apple into the lake until the basket
was empty again. From up above: *This whole
tree's crawling. Bring the ladder back.*

But I don't move, I sink into the water,
the whole summer soundless
and stripped around me.

My first conscious act of cruelty.
My clean back turned.

BEHIND THE BARN

Even if the ground is green,
you will be left alone. The smell

could be pine or mulch, it could
be early spring or late fall. If you

have loved, love will fall between
the words *lift up your hearts.* And

that will be all. Look at the bird
drowning in a bucket of water

while we sit on short wooden
stools braiding the divided world

that always comes undone.

IN THE LAKE

That was true love.
My mouth up against
a rowboat's quivering shadow,
water-reeds feathering
my wrists, knees.

The world was deaf.
A deceiving kingdom
on a mountain. The rock was cold
and blind, I flashed past
like a winged trout.

I reached, and could
only touch water's
flawless muscle. Then my lungs
gave in, silence replaced
by dry blue.

Love leads to mouthfuls
of unwanted air. Love
leads to lamenting the body's
buoyancy, the barely
explored depths.

ON LEARNING THE KNIFE

If you rub a just-picked apple on your sleeve
it shines like a hunter's moon.

And then, with a pocketknife he'd
split a fat one in half, dig out the core,
scatter the seeds, and hand me the flesh.

And it was what I expected. A fair
harvest, some perfect parts
mixed with whole sections of bruise.

That fall, the crisp days were filled
with light, like sipping river water from
your hand's mild cup.

Mealy days quickly followed and
were like swamps,
difficult to escape.

By the end of the season,
we were both astonished at how
effortlessly the blade cut through,

as if the skin put up no resistance,
the red fruit collapsing at
the slightest touch.

TO MYSELF

You are thankful for the chill,
the abundant trees losing frills just as you
seem to shed unnecessary parts. A finger
to a metal sliver, your torso in a dream.

You will not say *there are mistakes I have made.*
You will not say *goddamn this unholy world.*

Nothing is even, the scale tips to the right
or left depending on the wind, depending
on coins held too long in a moist palm.

No one receives a trophy for regret.
How obvious. Can't you think in subtleties?
Can't you learn to love loss
as St. Francis loved his Lady Poverty,
his rough brown tunic of discipline?

HIS REGRET

I thought we had what we needed.
A little path through the orchard,
leaves like a vast
green umbrella above.

For a while, the world appeared kind.
Water in the lake was warm as steam.
Salmonberries grew in great clumps
just beyond the last line of trees.

We'd lift the berries to our mouths,
one after the other, and the next
day there would be more.
A ripe, restless forest.

You know how it is—the moon looks
even more perfect with its cheek
pressed up against the sky
and the sky, that exact blue.

And like those too fat bees,
mindless on the sugar of apples
too long on the branch,
I said love without fury,

simply a movement of the tongue.
An offering of air. Clipped tulips
too long in the sun. And
that was all. Bones in a closed wing.

LATE DECEMBER

Motel signs announce winter rates,
free cable, clean rooms, and you
are tempted to crawl in, to say yes
to the silence, the anonymous white
sheets pulled up around your neck.

The kind snow throws itself down,
mouths: you don't need to see.

TREE

Look. February.
Love falls between the words
Lift up your hearts.
We lift them up.
Let us give thanks.

Until all is stark and you
swear you never believed
anyway.

THREE

*This sadness, holding you
while your wings diminish*

Lisel Mueller

DESCARTES AND REMBRANDT AT A DUTCH
SLAUGHTERHOUSE IN NINE BRUSHSTROKES

I.

Burnt orange

Descartes comes to the slaughterhouse to drag away bags of bones.
It is late in the day (he never rises from bed before noon) and he will
use the bones to study the body's form. The map beneath skin.
He gets used to the sour smell as his mind warms with the idea of
death. Light strikes his forehead from a high window, the carcasses
glow with a warm orange sheen:
all these bodies severed from the brain.

2.

More orange

Rembrandt comes to the building for the orange lustre and shadows
that fall between flesh. He brings a folder of paper and sits on a
wooden chair sketching the hanging bodies, the sharp movements of
men who cut into animal bellies with long-handled knives.
They are used to him now. No one even notices the man who draws
with quick hands.
Even quicker eyes.

3.

Maroon

Descartes: *I begin with what is around me. Clouds. Angles. Marrow.*
To explain the vastness he studies optics, mathematics, the gradual
movement of the moon.
He wanders. Looks for the snags in God's world.

4.

Bone white

Rembrandt leans over and sees a man with a burlap sack thrown over his shoulder.
He sketches that man walking from the building into early night, he tries to draw the sound of the man's footsteps and the shards of bone rubbing together with each step.
That sound is his portrait.

5.

Grey

Both want to know the smoothness of human beings and their thorns. Both work with light and shade.

6.

Yellow

Dogs howl outside the gates of the slaughterhouse.
Their eyes wolf-yellow.
Famished, they stalk the perimeter waiting for a man to throw a cow's heart over the fence. They fight for the meat. Rembrandt thinks that he comes from the same godly darkness where dogs exist. When he paints himself, he is almost entirely in shadow, God's yellow light across his face.

7.

Blue-green

Descartes switches slaughterhouses like he switches homes.
Street to street, country to country. He doesn't want visitors.
So he walks the outskirts of the city to find new gut-flecked floors.
He walks under a blue sky and some days it is like a dream; the
glass of his eyes looking at the sky, then again at the ground.

8.

White

Rembrandt: *I draw these suspended bodies over and over. Here, I am
close to God. Here, I am most aware of His spark in me.*
He comes for the shapes and the way gravity moulds muscle.
The puddles of blood on the sawdust floor are like paint on canvas.
The red spots seem to tell him: *a painting bleeds.*

9.

Absolute white

Descartes walks home in the dark. It is quiet. No trumpets or birds
sound. The air clears of the scent of blood as he picks through the
bones and lays them on paper covering his table.
He and the earth spin.

SNAPSHOTS OF DESCARTES IN SWEDEN

And the sill, where the absence of light
meets the absence of sound

Joanna Goodman

from a distance (evening)

Two silences: snow falling on a desert of snow and
wind that keeps them from speaking. The sky seems
all prayer and contemplation. In the distance a faint
outline of structure. *My warm room*, Descartes thinks.
He is sitting on the left of the sleigh, leaning his head
back as if to taste the whole sky. His new student,
Queen Kristina, looks straight ahead. They seem to
be floating across a wide vessel of glass. Into his chest
wind blows hard. This country is crystal. Vaguely blue.

Stockholm, October, 1649

from behind (morning)

He and Kristina ride away from the palace on two
chestnut horses. The Queen is asking something about
Aristotle, Descartes is turning his head to answer. They
walk each morning at 5. The sound of the hoofs on snow
is a strange colour Descartes has never seen before. He
imagines a stroke of hot sun finding the ground in front
of them. If in Holland he would wake 7 hours from now.
Eyes dark with sleep. Fingers, looped around the reins, on
fire. *Thoughts freeze here in winter just like the water.*

Stockholm, October, 1649

detail of: from behind (morning)

In the upper right corner a tangle of naked trees.
When Descartes sees them he will think of numbers.
Their perfectly smooth bodies. He will speak to
Kristina of soul and structure but he will be
thinking of an olive orchard he visited as a child.
The pale green pips spooned from vats inside the
caretakers' house, coarse against his tongue.

Stockholm, October, 1649

close-up

Descartes' left hand in his right. His knuckles
are raw roots. He will draw them up to his lips
and blow on them before putting on his fur
gloves. The paper in front of him is blank. Save
for a small drawing in the lower left corner.
It is an inky sketch of his flower garden in Holland.
A perfect line of bells on straight stalks.

Stockholm, November, 1649

from a high window looking down (mid-morning)

Descartes dismounting. The sky has lightened
slightly since they began their lesson two hours
ago. Kristina remains on her horse. She will ride
along the fence-line again thinking of her teacher's
last words: *only certainty can serve as a basis for knowledge.*
Descartes could be in the back corner of a Rembrandt
painting. His face a smudged slate. Absent. He looks
up to the watcher in the sky before hurrying inside.

Stockholm, November, 1649

from above (night)

In bed with his eyes open. His body is tired from
coughing. His hand on his chest is moist from
touching his forehead. Beyond the roof, stars.
Dear M. Descartes, Thank you for accepting my invitation
to visit Sweden. I am most eager to discuss your notions
of an infinite God and creation. In this dark he is certain
that all he knows wouldn't produce even a spark in the
frigid night. He thinks of nothing but heat. In two
hours he must rise. No amount of fur can warm him.

Stockholm, December, 1649

from the dining-room doorway (evening)

Descartes and Kristina sit at either end of
a wooden table. Sliced meat fans out on a
platter between them. They use the words:
certainty, passion, Galileo. The Queen tells Descartes
he looks unwell and urges him to sleep tomorrow.
He braces himself for the cold trip to his room.

Stockholm, January, 1650

close-up

It's as if the blood has been
drained from his cheeks.

His lips are plum shadows.

Stockholm, February, 1650

through a thick curtain of ice (night)

His lungs are a tangle of fishhooks.
Even now he longs for spring. Rain.
The room is dark, the curtains pulled.
A woman on a chair holds his hand
in hers. He is unsure of how to remain
whole. The last breath is a sort of
metallic tearing. The liquid pools and rests.

Stockholm, February, 1650

Four

There can be little doubt that in many ways the story of bridge building is the story of civilization. By it, we can readily measure an important part of a people's progress.

Franklin D. Roosevelt (October, 1931)

...it is perhaps not surprising that the most common fear among San Franciscans is gephyrophobia, the fear of crossing bridges.

Tad Friend (October, 2003)

SELF DECEIT

Until a friend moved to San Francisco,
that paper-lantern city of hills and ocean,
I couldn't imagine a fear of crossing.
Fear of the red limbed bridge that stretches
across foggy mornings, a fear of
the furrowed distance beneath. But he
confided over the phone that after only
a month of driving he no longer looks right
or left. Imagine, a sturdy structure, a happy man,
hands curled around the steering wheel like
pale pythons, his eyes only straight ahead.

They say it's like a gangway that, at once,
tongues both the edge of this golden continent
and the expanse beyond, a place one hangs
and asks the obvious: would it be like flying?
Like taking a deep breath before being swallowed,
a wet mouth as warm as sunned-upholstery,
as conclusive as sex? Certainly nothing about
the ribs snapping inward, lungs and heart punctured,
the spine, only shards and splinters.

I thought I was attuned to the music of fear.
But perhaps I know nothing of the need to rise,
the movements of those haunted by waters.

PONTE VECCHIO

From here the world is wet and broken
in two. From one side

      to the other wind brings speckled birds,
      damp wool, dust from

the jeweler's tiny knives. *Listen closely and the Arno*
loses its way

      like the quiet priest, hands tightly wrapped
      in white towels so as he threw

himself from the cobbled edge he wouldn't
bring his bare palms together to pray.

      Vecchio- aged, old,
      as in: *Il vecchio castello sta crollando.*

But not only the old castle, also the brother
of the priest who gave up

      half the city for fear of the rippled river,
      its sleepless need for the sea.

The priest was the only thing that fell that night.
The German soldiers forgot

      this city's stone rib as they retreated, they
      left it stretched across, unfailingly alive—

THE ARCHANGEL GABRIEL IN CONVERSATION

*(first third of the 14th century, embroidered in silk
and metal thread, 5 x 30 inches)*

Honey, last night I dreamed of you.   I was
supposed to tell you something but the words
slid down my polished throat and so I let
you do all the talking.   You seemed a little
sad.   Is it that loneliness again?   I
understand.   Sometimes the sky peels
away from me too.   Have you been sleeping
well?   Your eyes look glassy.   I have a
good feeling about this upcoming year.   Let's
not dwell on the past.   Let's count our
blessings the way we count the star's metal
bodies.   Mary.   I love that name.   Joyful.
There's that smile again.

THE POEM AS SAMURAI

Dangers are seasonal: too much green, too little.

If only the blade could open the belly without the
mess. As if the hole could gently speak of bees
and hard blue skies.

In your humble house imagine invisible walls.
Words moving in every direction forever.

The great mountain is not as high as it looks. On
the way up, notice the frilled apple blossom and the
worm as one in the same.

When the bandits come have no regard for future.
Watch with the muscles in your back.

Do not love so dearly
silk against the upper thigh
that you would not be prepared
to cast it off,
to feel the frozen brace of wind.

In the barren months go to the pot of rice,
level a cup, put the lid back on. Ask for a
bountiful harvest.

Originally there is nothing. The blank page.
*And my new Reader will come to me empty-
handed.* Lean your sword against the wall
a moment. Offer what you have. Then
turn and walk away.

FRATRES PONTIFICES

*In the early Middle Ages the Brotherhood of Bridgebuilders knit
together civilization with those indispensable stitches called bridges.*
        -Scott Corbett

Like kneeling in a chapel,
a bridge, too, offers
safe passage.

Wooden beams on stone piers
were an answered prayer,
a way to manage the horse,
as well as the swarming
cutthroats.

Perhaps those blessed with
dry feet planted firmly
on the other side thought:
*And God too must
have fastened bridges.*

MY BROTHER DIVES FROM THE CHRISTINA LAKE TRAIN BRIDGE

because even in this early light, the world's
thirst is clear. Everything points skyward,
waiting for a downpour,

a long drink at the well. And like the pine's head
reaching for tossed cloud, my brother, too,
launches himself from the

ground. He tucks his head between his arms,
which are straight and at his ears and then plunges
into the blonde water,

his feet still ringing from a moment on the metal
ledge. And when he hangs there he knows the earth
is severed from the sky,

the rip as long as the longest breath. And without
breath the fissure closes, the body and sky fused.
Both without weight or

message, he waits as long as he can
before returning to shore.

ACROSS THE DARDANELLES

(5th century BC)

Furious weather destroyed the partially
      built pontoon bridge, 674 boats long, that Xerxes
            was throwing from Persia to Greece

        and in his anger, the ruler punished the sea
    with 300 lashes and a pair of manacles to curb the manners
                of that wet spirit.

          The logs and cables were refastened,
    brushwood and bulwarks screened the horses from
        the field of ocean beside, as for seven days and nights

two million men crossed, then returned
      as their might surged,
             then waned.

        At the hinge where land and water met Xerxes stood
and watched the defeat, the falling sun glinting off helmets,
            then drifting darkness presented

        as an amulet,
    or the nimble hands of builders.

CONSTRUCTION

Calculate the forces: bridges' weight, traffic's load, wind,
earthquake, water.

Remember that tension and compression are opposites.
Shear means cutting through, *torsion* is the force of twisting.

Stone is good. Vines and ropes, as well.
Don't use balsa. A stout trunk of oak is more durable.
Iron and steel, the best.

Find the spot on which you will build. Name it *protection,
balance, parade route.*

If you desire something grander, more elegant,
consider suspension.
It will appear gravity-defying, a leap into the unknown,
but it is still beam and arch. Still dependent on two
opposite points.

Under your breath don't hum:
London Bridge is falling down, falling down, falling down
because it didn't.

A TURNER EXHIBIT AT THE TATE

For Deirdre

The whole thing made me dizzy. Seasick,
I think, though as a child I'd been known
for my sea-legs, the only one in my family

who didn't blush green on the rough winter
ferry trip from the mainland to the island.
When Deirdre and I arrived at the gallery that

morning we'd thought it would be an escape from
the expensive streets, weather, the sharp coiled
spring that shot through the mattress and ripped

finger-size holes in my pajama-bottoms. But
after shuffling through countless rooms stacked
from waist to ceiling with seascapes and seasonal

fields, I longed for anything with a face, for a lone
painting on a wide white wall. There were so
many rooms and hallways and rows of gold frames

I could hardly believe one person was
responsible for them all. At some point we
lost each other and eventually made

our separate ways to the postcard-stand meeting
place on the first floor where we sat on the stairs
watching a long line snake towards the washrooms

and two guards outside the glass doors on their
smoke-break. *I need a drink*, so we lifted our
coats over our shoulders, opened a big black umbrella
and left Turner's stormy world for our own.

ODE TO RAFFLESIA

For Suzanne

I, too, am weary of poems
         for flowers.   Weary of grape-
            vines and panorama, of
                moon in water, pine and

birch.   Yesterday, I would not
         have written to you with
            a title such as, *Ode to Rafflesia*—

ode to anything— certainly
         not in praise of the growing,

the bits of senseless seed
         dirty and tangled beneath
         this quilted skirt of interminable

         snow.

         Rafflesia, dogged parasite,

digs its teeth into tender
         grape-vines and sucks.   Bloated
            as round as a basketball,

         it smells like a forest of
            manure, procreates because

blueblack flies believe the petals
         are hunks of decaying flesh.

         Anything to counter feathers
            and apples.   Anything asking
            asylum from the beautiful.

GALLOPING GERTIE

(Tacoma Narrows, Washington, 1940)

And she galloped right out of the sky.

Wind lifting her concrete body in great bucks,
the architects and builders shamefaced,
chewing their soft lips.

She broke. Withdrew from the mathematical
equations meant to explain the world, the steel knuckles
meant to hold it. As if anything can be held,
or remedied, explained with equations written

across the page; suspended across Puget Sound.
Someone puts the disaster remnants in pleasing
groupings under glass. Mounts bright bulbs to
illuminate the shattered pieces, there is a video

that plays over and over. And each time
she twists and buckles in black and white, breaks
in half. The lone car with the dog, frantic
at each window, plunges into the cold water that
seems to gesture, come down. The man on the edge, safe,

reaches for nothing, the whole failed day at his feet.

SELF DECEIT

For Curt Lush

The body can survive
the unspeakable.
You waited years
then finally lay
down as the half-light
of rescue receded.
You sang:
Toronto smells
of neglect.

Sometimes
all is earthbound.
Swarms of yellowjackets
abandon the park's
garbage cans
and bury themselves
in the dirt.
Rivers slow their
charge and stare
at the bridges
stretched
above. Nothing
lingers on the birch
branches. You
knew it would hurt.

I thought I loved this world.
Fires started by a
spark from this or that
stone, sky bearded
in rain. But perhaps it is

foolish to desire
that which cannot
love back. That which
lifts and then
just lets a body fall.

THE DANCE OF DEATH BRIDGE

Lucerne (14th century)

The whole structure might have sunk
into the muck had it not been for that
perfectly simple geometric shape.

The triangle, a fool's knowledge of
tension and compression, and the
covered bridge remains.

When your eyes have adjusted,
look to the ceiling, to the painted
scenes of life's stages and in each

frame, death crouched on bony
haunches. A reminder perhaps that
currents shift and rivers reverse,

that the end becomes a beginning,
as the truss attempts to keep the body
from sinking, or going adrift.

BEETHOVEN CONDUCTING SYMPHONY NO. 9
ON MAY 7, 1824, IN VIENNA

In the thirteenth century, in the dark, monks read
by the light of their own bodies.

Like their denial of blindness, Beethoven hears
the stone light of the luminous music that is played.

After all, this is his heart,
his Godly parade.

UNNAMED

We too have our rivers for the damned.
When peering into water, whose face is reflected back at you?
          nathalie stephens

From this bridge the city sprawls like a body laid flat, not quite
breathing, not quite not. History gathers beneath, slips into
whirlpools, feverish names that disappear, then reappear on the
banks, like world-weary detritus. I won't mouth the obvious. The
ones N calls, *in Letters*. Their books in neat stacks on my desk.
Rivers imitate final sentences, rough and muffled. The bridged
Seine as grave. Nuremberg Bridge. The Ouse. Breath stops and
the city continues to glint and sparkle as if there's nothing wrong.
Nothing inside of it wrecked. As if *what survives burning drowns*.

THE POEM AS BREATHLESS FOOL

And who can blame
the heart for desiring
        the sleeve's flag.
The drunken arm raising a full glass
to love of everything: country,
lamp posts, plump blueberries,
        the dead.

In the rain
        light looks holy.
The fool unlocks the door
and wanders the streets
        naked watching slick
drops fall.
On the tongue,
fingertips taste of salt.

Everything is something
else. Love is this or
that flower, perhaps
        a heron.
Or bell. Someone
leans into someone else.
Someone sings
or rises.

PONT NEUF

*The New Bridge, the longest in Paris, was a cheerful place where one
was always sure to meet, at any hour, a monk, a white horse, and a
whore.*
    from "One History of Paris"

A forgotten dog tied too tightly around a chestnut
tree can't sit, so she circles long into the night

until the stiff rope frays and splits,
drags it behind her under the fence and away.

Beyond the fence is Paris, where a man
stands in front of a colour coded map and thinks

this is a city of bridges. A city severed in the middle,
a city of north and south. He lifts the idea of each

name to his mouth, *Pont Royal, Pont du Carrousel,
Pont des Arts,* and files them under *ways to deny*

the river. And then he finds the longest and
walks across. Is he different on the other side?

The world of the bridge has changed, no longer
a nightly meeting place of bear-trainers and fire-spitters,

teeth-pullers and monks reciting hurdy-gurdy
songs of the Middle Ages. No longer duels and

beheadings, entertainers applauded by a drunken
audience for their wild criticism of everything.

Now, though, past midnight, after too much wine,
someone quietly steps from the riverbank into the Seine,

thinking, *I swear this is where I left it, someone's moved the bloody bridge,* as if everything made tame still comes apart

in the dark. And the lost dog circles the statue of Henry IV
atop his bronze horse who has been still for centuries

lamely guarding this swath of river, watching the ruckus
and the silence. The written and the erased.

AFTER THE PARTY

Sometimes the world hangs quietly.
Across the wild lawn, guests
have disappeared,
as if it is only night they need
and not this wooden porch,
these four rooms.
And eventually everything leaves.
Haystacks. Plums.
The deaf family dog.
And this is how I prepare.
This is how I ready myself.

EARLY MARCH AND WE STOP IN A TOWN TOO SMALL FOR THE MAP SOMEWHERE NORTH OF THUNDER BAY

after Shane Rhodes

because the sky seems to say: *my pretty, my hollow one*

because a garden in full bloom can be so vulgar in its obviousness

because language can be whittled down to *stop* and *watch*

because you have never seen a moose

because light above those wispy pines is bent into a bow

because all we've been listening to since the Manitoba border is Glenn Gould

because we hurt here and here and here

because next summer in Montréal when the air conditioning refuses to work we will need a memory that recalls air as cold as this wind

because there must be more to this scene than *lonely*

because *Great stars of white frost / come with the fish of darkness / that opens the road of dawn*

because the sound of soles across frozen ground is as lovely as polished rosewood

because the sky seems to say: *my hollow one*

NOTES

The "Self Deceit" poems were inspired by a photograph by Francesca Woodman.

"First Day of Hunting Season" and parts of "Health" were both inspired by the tales of Megan Newell.

The epigraph for section two: *Sursum corda. Habemus ad Dominum!* means "Lift up your hearts. We have lifted them up to the Lord!"

Originally there is nothing in "The Poem as Samurai" is from the Platform Sutra of the Sixth Patriarch.

And my new Reader will come to me empty-handed in "The Poem as Samurai" is a line by Olena Kalytiak Davis.

The line *what survives burning drowns* in the poem "Unnamed" is from *Scène* by nathalie stephens.

The line in "Early March..." *Great stars of white frost / come with the fish of darkness / that opens the road of dawn* is by Lorca.

Thanks to the publications in which some of these poems have appeared: "A Drunk's Daughter" in the *Michigan Quarterly Review*, "After the Party" in the *Southern Indiana Review* and "Conversion," "The Poem as Samurai," "Ode to Rafflesia" and "Across the Dardanelles" in *The Southern Review*.

I am indebted to Donovan Hohn, Jessie Weise, Rachel Richardson, John Cox, Carrie Strand, Veronica Pasfield, Rachel Nelson, Matthew Hittinger, Sarah Evilsizor, Marika Ismail, Angela Lea, Sejal Sutaria, Scotti Parrish, Keith Taylor, Peter Ho Davies, and Andrea Beauchamp for two years of sustained growth.

My deep gratitude to Rachel Losh and Megan Newell for reading this work in its entirety and for their faithful windmill support.

Innumerable thanks to Thomas Lynch, Linda Gregerson, Richard Tillinghast, Lorna Goodison, Larry Goldstein, and Thylias Moss for all their wise words.

Thanks to Phillip Levine for his help with "Waking Early in a New House."

Thanks to Jim Reid for his very close reading of these poems.

Continued and constant thanks to Ray and Joyce Hancock, Suzanne Robertson, Brian Harrington, Deirdre Harrington, nathalie stephens, Jeff and Christy Topolewski-Hancock, Gladys and Wally Scott, Doug and Gloria Scott, Sharon Lee, Parissa, Payam, and Keon Madani, Manije and Gary Cohen, Lewis Melville, Susan Turner, Julie, Dean, Jack and Cole Shepard, Ray and Betty Brunelle, Adrienne Argent, Jan, Al and Greg Argent, Wendy, Marty and Aidan Tait-Sakich, Deane and Layne Williams, Janice Kulyk-Keefer, Laura Lush, Ardessa Jesseau, Mac, Matt Jones, and Misty Bergeron for their love and support.

Thank you so much to Denis De Klerck of Mansfield Press for believing in this work and for the time and effort put into making this book possible.

And always, for everything, Barzin Hosseini-Rad.

Suzanne Hancock lives and writes in Toronto. She recently
received an MFA in creative writing from the University
of Michigan.